Four Funerals and a Wedding

Four Funerals and a Wedding

A selection of quotes, quips and jokes collected by

DAVID PYTCHES

Cartoons by Taffy Davies

LEIGH ROAD
BAPTIST CHURCH
ESSEX

eagle

Guildford, Surrey

Text: Copyright © 1999 David Pytches
Cartoons: Copyright © 1999 Taffy Davies

The right of David Pytches to be identified as compiler of this work has been asserted by him in accordance with the Copyright, Design and Patents Act 1988.

British Library Cataloguing in Publication Data. A catalogue record for this book is available from the British Library.

Published by Eagle, an imprint of Inter Publishing Service (IPS) Ltd, PO Box 530, Guildford, Surrey GU2 5FH.

Typeset by Eagle Publishing
Printed by Gutenburg Press, Malta
ISBN No: 0 86347 346 6

DEATH AND FUNERALS

Notice in churchyard. Only the dead living in this parish may be buried here

The grass is always greener on the other fellow's grave.
(Spike Milligan)

Obituary of a much loved vicar: 'He was literally the father of all the children of the parish!'

If Churchill were alive today he'd turn over in his grave.

My wife died of asbestosis – it took two weeks to cremate her!

If at first you don't succeed – so much for sky diving!

Class distinction is only temporary.
All men are cremated equal. *(Chelsea wall graffiti)*

For Sale: Full length undertaker's coat – left shoulder slightly worn. £6. *(Chester Observer)*

A lawyer, who worked as a legal advisor to a businessman whom he distrusted, was rung up by the wife to tell him that her husband had had an accident and was dead.'Will you be coming to the funeral?' she asked. 'No!' replied the lawyer. 'I believe you.'

A man was just about to enter the gates of Heaven when St Peter stepped forward and stopped him: 'Sorry, but you've told too many lies to be permitted entry.'

'Come off it,' said the man, 'surely you have not forgotten that you were once a fisherman?'

Surprised to spot an empty seat in a packed stadium a fan commented on it to the woman seated nearby. 'It was my husband's,' she said. I'm so sorry,' said the man, 'but I am amazed that, on an occasion like this, one of his relatives or friends hasn't jumped at the chance to take his reserved seat.' 'That's what beats me too,' she replied, 'but they all insisted on going to his funeral.'

A musician's will: 'I leave my violins to the Royal Philharmonic Orchestra, my pianos to the Royal School of Music and my organs to the Royal College of Surgeons.' *(C. George)*

The widow learned, when hearing her late husband's will being read, that he had left the bulk of his fortune to another woman. She was so enraged that she rushed round to the stonemasons to change the inscription on her spouse's headstone. 'I'm so sorry madam, but you asked for "Rest in Peace" on your order and that is what has been inscribed. We can't change it now.' 'All right then,' she muttered indignantly, 'but just add after it: "Until We Meet Again!" '

The Irish Inquest Jury had debated the issue long and hard. A body had been found at the bottom of a cliff in the village. It was lunchtime and they were all hungry, so they brought the verdict of, 'An Act of God – in suspicious circumstances.'

11

Die, my dear doctor, that's the last thing I shall do!
(Lord Palmerston)

According to obituary notices a mean and useless citizen never dies

Notice: Keep death off the roads – drive on the pavement! *(graffiti)*

'Now tell me was it you or your brother who was killed in the war?'

If I could drop dead right now I'd be the happiest man alive. *(Samuel Goldwyn)*

Do you know it costs thousands of pounds to have a funeral today? That's why they refer to the deceased as the dear departed!

Mother turkey to baby turkeys misbehaving at Christmas time: 'If your father could see you now he'd be turning in his gravey.'

Three drunks were stumbling home late one night and took a short cut through a graveyard. One of them called to the others as he had just tripped over a headstone. 'Look, this says the deceased lived to the ripe old age of 95!'. Almost at once another shouted that he had just stumbled over a grave where the man was 104 when he died. By this time they were nearly on the road again when the third drunk called out, 'Come and have a look at this one – he was 145 years old!' The others were incredulous. 'What's his name?' asks the first one.

'Let's see!' says his friend, striking a light to see the inscription more clearly. 'It's Miles from Dublin.'

A violinist was advised by his surgeon that he'd have to undergo an operation.

'But, doctor,' the patient implored, 'I have important concerts booked ahead. If you operate, can I be assured that I'll be able to play the violin in two weeks time?'

'Undoubtedly!' assured the doctor. 'The last patient I operated on was playing a harp within twenty-four hours!'

They say that the traffic is so bad in Maidstone that a man is knocked down every day – and he is getting jolly well fed up with it.

It is not always easy to say the right thing on the spur of the moment. We can sympathise with the chap who met an old friend after many years.

'How's your wife?'

'She's in heaven,' replied the friend.

'Oh, I'm sorry,' stammered the chap. Then realising this was not the thing to say, stammered. 'I mean I'm glad.' That seemed even worse so he tried again, 'Well, what I really mean is, I'm surprised.'

A very elderly parson was waiting at the cemetery after a funeral at which he had officiated when the undertaker passed him with the comment: 'There's not much point in you going home really, is there Sir?' (*Hector Huxham*)

I'm not afraid to die; I just don't want to be there when it happens. *(Woody Allen)*

There are only two sorts of pedestrian in Paris – the quick and the dead!

The greatest problem in America today is procrastination. Take funerals! Why do people wait till the last minute to have them?

She was never really charming until she died.
(Terence)

'Did he go to church?' enquired the undertaker. 'No!' said the widow.

'Did he belong to Rotary?'

'No!'

'Did he belong to the Freemasons or the Knights of Columbus?'

'No! No! No!'

'Was he a member of the Ku-Klux-Klan?

'What's that?' asked the widow

'That's one of those devils under the sheets,' explained the undertaker.

'Yes! That was him exactly!'

A man opened a newspaper and was amazed to read his own obituary. Much amused, he telephoned his best friend who asked him where he was ringing from!

'I've never wanted to see anybody die, but there are a few obituary notices I have read with pleasure.' *(Clarence Darrow)*

Two ghosts meet in a lonely corridor at the dead of night. One greets the other, 'Hi Bill! Are you all right? You look like nothing on earth!'

A man's mother-in-law passed on and his wife asked him what sort of gravestone they should get her.
'Something very, very heavy,' he replied.

Voter: Why, I wouldn't vote for you if you were St Peter himself!
Candidate: If I were St Peter, you couldn't vote for me – you wouldn't be in my constituency.

Priest: Do you want to go to heaven?
Irish parishioner: No Father.
Shocked priest: But you must want to go to heaven when you die.
Irish parishioner: Oh, yes, when I die, Father. I thought you were getting a party together now.

I don't mind dying; the trouble is you feel so stiff the next day. *(George Axlerod)*

My friend, the undertaker, the last person on earth to let me down.

You know I'm worried. Yesterday I caught the bouquet at the funeral!

The reports of my death have been greatly exaggerated. *(Mark Twain)*

I would like to live in Manchester, England. The transition between Manchester and death would be unnoticeable. *(Mark Twain)*

Secondhand tombstone for sale. Ideal for person named O'Reilly. *(Advertisement in a Dublin newspaper)*

I don't believe in dying. It's been done. I'm working on a new exit. Besides, I can't die now – I'm booked. *(George Burns)*

The realisation that one is to be hanged in the morning concentrates the mind wonderfully.
(Samuel Johnson)

Did you hear about the undertaker who concludes all his demand letters with: 'Yours eventually'?

They say such nice things about people at their funerals that it makes me sad to realise that I'm going to miss mine by just a few days.
(Garrison Keillor)

The vicar was doing his regular rounds in his rural parish and was disturbed by the smell of a dead donkey rotting at the road side which remained unattended for days. Other parishioners were also complaining to him about it. Finally the vicar wrote a little note to the Parish Council, drawing attention to the situation. The Council replied that they had always assumed it was the duty of the vicar to bury all the dead in the parish!

The vicar replied that he was well aware of his duty but it had always been his practice to inform the relatives first!

First elderly vicar at fraternal: Heard you had to bury your rural dean!
Second elderly vicar: Yes, we had to you know – he died!

As he was lowering the body into its last resting place, the respected grave-digger suddenly collapsed and died, which event cast a gloom over the entire proceedings. *(Bernard Falck)*

If you don't go to other men's funerals, they won't go to yours. *(Clarence S. Day)*

He was a great patriot, a humanitarian, a loyal friend – provided of course he really is dead.
(Voltaire)

The reason why so many people showed up at Louis B. Mayer's funeral was because they wanted to make sure he was dead. *(Samuel Goldwyn)*

The following are taken from inscriptions on gravestones:

In this grave here do I lie
Back to back my wife and I
When the last trump the air shall fill
If she gets up, I'll just lie still.

Here lies James Burke
A decent man entirely.
We bought this tombstone second-hand,
and his name's not Burke, it's Riley.

Here lies my wife.
Here let her lie!
Now she's at rest, And so am I. *(John Dryden)*

Benjamin Franklin composed his own epitaph for his tombstone:

The body
of
Benjamin Franklin
Printer
(Like the cover of an old book,
Its contents torn out
And stript
Of its lettering and guilding)
Lies here food for worms
But the work itself
Shall not be lost
For it will, as he believed
Appear once more
In a new
And more elegant edition
Revised and corrected
by
The Author

27

A graveyard inscription supposed to be in a Woolwich church graveyard ran:

Sacred
to the memory
of
Major James Brown
who
was killed by the
accidental discharge
of a pistol by his batman

Well done thou good and faithful servant

A tombstone found in Stepney, London:

Whoever treadeth on this stone
I pray you tread most neatly
For underneath this same do lie
Your honest friend—
WILL WHEATLEY
Ob November 10 1683

Lord she is thin. *(It is said that this epitaph appears at the bottom of a Tasmanian tombstone. The 'e' is on the back, the stonemason not having left himself enough room to engrave it on the front.)*

A tombstone found in Hastings, Sussex:

16 Jany 1751

Joseph Bain

Good peppell as you pass by
I pray you on me cast
an I
For as you am so wounce Wous I
And as i am so must
you be
Therefor prepare to
follow me

There was an old fellow of Hyde
Who fell down a manhole and died
He had a young brother
Who fell down another
And now they're interred side by side

When Archdeacon Palmer was a curate he set off for a funeral on his bicycle, but being overtaken by the hearse he put more pressure on the pedals and the chain broke. Desperate that he might be very late he hailed a vehicle passing by which happened to be a dustcart. The driver responded magnificently and the dustcart arrived just a second ahead of the hearse. Congratulated with hearty cheers from the dustmen, Palmer slipped in, robed and without delay led the mourners into the service. He wondered whatever they must be thinking when he found himself uttering the lines 'Dust thou art and to dust thou shalt return!'

One man greeted another with the words, 'Hello, George, I thought you were dead.' The other man replied firmly, 'No, I'm not dead.' 'Oh dear!' said the first man. 'If you're not dead, whose funeral did I go to last February?'

A parachutist was appalled to discover when he had jumped from the plane that his rip-cord did not work. As he gathered momentum descending to earth, he passed another man coming up. 'Hi there! Do you know anything about parachutes?' 'Sorry!' shouted back the man coming up. 'Do you know anything about gas cookers?'

One night a courting couple spotted a ghostly figure in the moonlight crouching by a tombstone. Their attention was drawn to it by a constant chipping sound – the impact of a mallet and chisel. Catching the ghost by surprise, they asked, 'What's going on here?' The ghost suddenly disappeared complaining, 'They've spelt my name wrong!'

The vicar was trying to impress upon his congregation the seriousness of life. 'Do you realise that everyone in this parish is going to die!' A man near the front began smiling very obviously.

The vicar, thinking that he could not have heard what had been said the first time, repeated his solemn statement.

The man smiled again; indeed he almost laughed.

The vicar felt he had to challenge him from the pulpit. 'Why did you look so happy when I said that?'

'Well,' replied the man, 'I'm just so happy that I don't live in this parish!'

A pessimist is a man who, when he smells flowers, looks around for the coffin. *(H.L. Mencken)*

Any man's death diminishes me, because I am involved in Mankind; and therefore never send to know for whom the bell tolls; It tolls for thee. *(John Donne)*

The vicar's small daughter was seen burying a dead bird in the garden: 'In the Name of the Father, and of the Son, and into the hole he goes. Amen.'

The vicar had to bury a local scoundrel and was hard put to find anything good to say about the deceased. He consulted the rural dean who told him he would simply have to wait for some spontaneous inspiration at the graveside, as he really had no idea what he could say.

When it was time for his address, the vicar began, 'I can't say much for his relationship with his mother. She committed suicide through drink; nor for his wife who divorced him; nor for his children who can't be here because all three are in prison for mugging; or even of his neighbours who constantly complained to the police about him; but what I can say is that compared to his brother he was a saint.'

Q: Why are there so few men with whiskers
in heaven?
A: Because most men get in by a close shave.

She was a town-and-country soprano of the kind
often used for augmenting grief at a funeral.
(George Ade)

A cemetery is the dead centre of the town

DOCTORS, DISEASES AND HOSPITALS

Doctor: Your cough is a little better today.
Student: It ought to be. I've been practising all night.

My doctor gave me six months to live, but when I couldn't pay he gave me six months more. *(Walter Matthau)*

The best medical speciality is dermatology. Your patients never call you out in the middle of the night, they never die of the disease, and they never get any better. *(Martin H. Fischer)*

Hypochondria is the one disease I haven't got.

After two days in hospital, I took a turn for the nurse. *(Rodney Dangerfield)*

The operation was a complete success, but the patient died of something else. *(John Chiene)*

Notice in Watford Journal: A healing session by Mr R.U. Well has been cancelled owing to illness.

A new young nurse was on the ward for the first time and arrived on duty one evening to find a little old lady sitting by the first bed. Checking her notes the nurse asked her to come now and have her bath.

Looking puzzled the old lady protested softly: 'But I have already had mine today.'

'No dear, you're getting confused. Come along now,' the nurse insisted firmly.

The old lady meekly complied and went off with the nurse for a bath.

Bath finished, the nurse proceeded to help her back to the ward.

Nearing her bed, the nurse turned to her in surprise and said, 'Who is that, dear, in your bed?' 'Oh,' said the little old lady. 'That's my sister! I came here to visit her!'

A vicar's wife took her husband for a medical check-up following a severe attack on his health. After examining the vicar, the doctor calls the wife into his office and tells her: 'Your husband is suffering from a very serious disease, combined with stress which could kill him in a few months. What you have to do is, each morning, fix him with a nice breakfast, and be very pleasant to him. Always cook him meals you know he enjoys and don't expect him to help around the house or garden or with the children – especially after a hard day in the parish. And don't burden him with too many of your own problems because that will only increase the stress. And most importantly, make love to him a couple of times a week. If you can do this for the next ten months, I think your husband could well pull through completely.'

On the way home the vicar asked his wife what the doctor had said?

His wife replied: 'The doctor said you are going to die!'

WEDDINGS

I married Miss Right. I just didn't know her first name was 'Always'.

A man is incomplete until he is married and then he's finished!

She took him for better or for worse, but unfortunately he was worse than she took him for.

'If we did become engaged would you give me a ring?' she said. 'Yes! Sure! What is your number?'

To keep your marriage brimming
With love in the loving cup,
If ever you're wrong, admit it,
If ever you're right, shut up!
(Ogden Nash)

They say he married her because her aunt left her a fortune. He hotly denies it, saying he would have married her whoever had left her the fortune.

Signing the register at a wedding, the best man had difficulty on making his ball-point pen work. 'Put your weight on it,' said the vicar. He signed it: 'John Smith (Eleven stone four pounds).'

An Irish lawyer was once asked if he knew what the penalty was for bigamy. 'Yes,' he replied, 'two mothers-in-law.'

'And where are you going for your honeymoon?' enquired the vicar, kindly, as the new couple finished signing the vestry registers. 'Belgium,' replied the bride. 'Antwerp?' asked the vicar who had once served as a chaplain there. 'Oh yes!' she replied. 'I am taking my husband with me.'

'Sir, I wish to marry your daughter.'
'Can you support a family?' enquired the prospective father-in-law.
'Yes sir, I think so.'
'Good! There are eight of us.'

Some people ask the secret of our long marriage. We take time to go to a restaurant twice a week. A little candlelight dinner, soft music and a slow walk home. She goes on Tuesdays; I go on Fridays.

Two newly-weds rode off on their horse through the forest. They hadn't gone far when the horse stumbled. 'That's once!' said the groom sternly. They travelled on for a further distance and the horse stumbled again. 'That's twice!' said the groom very sternly. They travelled on together for a few more miles, when finally the horse stumbled yet more and the groom took out his gun and shot it! The bride was horrified and remonstrated with him for destroying their only means of transport.

'That's once!' said the groom.

Said the parson at the wedding
'Don't be nervous for you see
Everything that's said or done
You say and do it after me.'

'Wilt thou take and wed this woman?
And endeavour to be true?'
But the bridegroom much embarrassed
Only stammered, 'After you!'

A businessman called in on a married couple that he had known as friends for many years. He was impressed by a new attitude they seemed to have towards each other. The man was so tender and considerate. The visitor was curious: 'Hey! What's happened to you two? Your marriage seems to be working out much better than when I was last here.' 'Oh yes,' the husband replied, 'we've been on one of those Marriage Encounter programmes and it's helped us so much. In fact we have some brochures here and we would be happy for you and your wife to go on one at our expense.' 'Oh no, thanks very much,' said the visitor, 'I think I've got the message all right.'

On arriving home, instead of the usual peck on the cheek, monosyllabic greeting, falling into his chair and becoming totally fixated by the TV, he took his wife in his arms and settled her gently down beside him. 'Now darling,' he began, in the most considerate, tender tone he could muster, 'don't worry about the meal for the moment as I feel it would be so nice if we could prepare the food together later. Just tell me what kind of a day you've had instead of my boring you with all our office frustrations. What's been happening and who have you talked to today? I've been thinking about you so much, and what an adorable wife you are to me and wondering how its been for you. I've also bought some wine . . .' At this point his wife suddenly burst into tears. This not being at all the way he had imagined it would work out the husband was quite taken aback.

'Whatever's wrong?' he sighed. 'Well I've had a simply awful day,' she sobbed. 'My friend is upset with me, the baby has been crying all day, the dog has been sick on our best carpet – and now you come home drunk!'

'It does not matter how often a married man changes his job he always ends up with the same boss.'

Husband: 'I was a fool when I married you.'
Wife: 'Yes dear. I was so much in love that I didn't notice.'

'Do you have the book *Man, Master of Women*?' a young man asked the lady librarian.
'Fiction counter to your left,' the librarian replied nonchalantly.

Marriage: it starts when you sink into his arms and ends with your arms in the sink.

At her wedding, the bride tripped and fell into the arms of the vicar. 'That's the first time I've held a fallen woman,' he quipped. To which she retorted: 'It's the first time I've been picked up by a vicar!'

The couple were on their honeymoon in Italy and the newly married groom wished to impress his bride at the restaurant. After choosing the wine he picked up the menu and asked for Ignacio Garibaldi Especalucci. The waiter looked at him rather puzzled: 'I'm sorry Signor but that's the proprietor!'

A couple in Hollywood got divorced. Then they got remarried. The divorce didn't work out!

A bachelor instructed his computer to come up with a perfect mate who would be very sociable, loved swimming, was small and would cause every one to gasp in amazement.

The computer soon came back with the answer: 'Marry a penguin!'

Married to an absent-minded professor, the wife rushed to the door of his study: 'Darling!' she called out, 'have you remembered that it was thirty years ago today that you asked me to marry you?'

The professor looked up with a creased brow muttering: 'And did you?'

It was an Italian wedding and when it came to the vows the priest put the usual question to the bride: 'Do you take Franco Miguel Hipolito to be your wedded husband?'

The bride appeared flustered. 'Father!' she said, 'there must be a mistake. I'm only meant to be marrying Frank!'

There was this Spanish Catholic girl named Carmen Gonzales who married a Jew called Hymie Cohen. They had no problems about an interfaith marriage. Hymie was insistent that his wife should follow hers but he wanted her also to accompany him each Sabbath to the synagogue. She found her weekends very busy – in fact from Friday till Sunday lunchtime she really didn't know whether she was Carmen or Cohen.

A couple went to the divorce court. He was 93 and they had been married for 73 years.

'Why give it up now?' asked the judge sadly.

'Well, your Honour,' replied the wife, 'our marriage has been on the rocks for years but we agreed to put off divorce until the children were all dead!'

Son to father: 'Does it cost a lot to get married?'
Father: 'Don't know, son, I'm still paying for it.'

A couple, just married, got among their wedding gifts a couple of tickets to a very fine show with the mysterious words 'Guess who?' scribbled across them. They went to the show but when they returned they found all their wedding presents were gone and another note in the same writing saying, 'Now you know!'

A female relative arrived late for the wedding and wanted to know all about it. 'Who gave the bride away?' She was shocked by what she heard: 'Well any one of us could have done but we all agreed to keep our mouths shut!'

First foreigner: My wife has no children. She impregnable!
Second foreigner: No! No! No! That's not right! You mean your wife is inconceivable!
Third foreigner: Excuse me but that's not right either. I think you mean your wife is unbearable!

Make love not war – I'm married and I do both.
(Barbara Kelly)

Their marriage is a wonderful partnership –
he's the silent partner!

Las Vegas is filled with all kinds of gambling
devices – dice tables, slot machines and
wedding chapels!

Anytime you see a young man opening the door of his car for his girlfriend you know that either the car is new or the girlfriend is.

Usher at wedding: 'Are you a friend of the groom?' 'Certainly not. I'm the bride's mother!'

The bride wept. The bridesmaids wept. Even the wedding cake was in tiers!

I know a guy who wants to get married but he can't. He's a pacifist!

Wedding Telegrams

To the bride: 'Congratulations from your loving mother on your wedding. Twenty years ago I sent you to bed with a dummy and tonight history repeats itself.'

To the groom from your new in-laws: 'Be careful! She spends money like water but that is her only extravagance!'

To the groom: 'Congratulations from the Maffioso. We have just kidnapped your new mother-in-law. If you don't pay the ransom immediately we will send her back!'

Nowadays two can live as cheaply as one large family used to! *(Joey Adams)*

Often the difference between a successful marriage and a mediocre one consists in leaving about three or four things unsaid. *(Harlan Miller)*

Son: 'Dad I heard that in some parts of Africa a man does not know his wife until he marries her.'
Father: 'That happens in most parts of the world, my son.'

The tongue-tied vicar addressed a wedding couple standing before him in the church: 'I require and charge you both . . . if either of you know any impediment why ye may not be jawfully loined together in matrimony ye do now confess it . . .'

The nervous groom placed the ring on the bride's finger and the vicar had just reached the part where he quietly instructed the groom to repeat what the vicar was saying: 'Now say everything after me in a nice strong voice!' At this point the vicar suddenly noticed that the groom was no longer holding the ring on the bride's finger so he whispered, 'Hold it on.' The obedient groom responded and called, 'Hold it on!' in a bold voice to everyone's mystification.

The vicar said: 'Do you promise to obey?'
The bride said: 'Do you think I'm crazy?'
The groom said: 'I do.'

'Did you hear about the man that had three wives in three months? The first two died of poisoned mushrooms.'
'What happened to the third wife?'
'She died from a blow on the head. She wouldn't eat the mushrooms!'

A good marriage would be between a blind wife and deaf husband. (*Michel de Montaigne*)

I proposed to my wife in the garage and couldn't back out

The couple had made their vows and the vicar had pronounced the couple man and wife. He then blessed them as they knelt at the chancel steps. After that he told them to follow him as he processed quite a little distance to the communion rails. When he turned to face the couple to pray for them he saw they had followed him up on their knees! Well, what was done was done so discreetly he drew no attention to it. But when the prayer was over and the couple stood up to follow him out to the vestry for signing the register, the bride displayed two ugly great floor polish stains on the front of her beautiful wedding dress!

Complete in her wedding gown the bride confronted her cricket-mad fiance.

'How could you do it? There I was waiting at the church with all my relatives and friends and where were you? Playing cricket! You left me in the lurch!'

He tried to calm her down. 'I distinctly said: If it rains . . .'

Wife: 'My husband wears the pants in our family, but I tell him which pants to wear.'

Judge: Have you ever been cross examined before?
Accused: Yes, your honour! I am a married man.

You have to kiss an awful lot of frogs before you find a prince. *(Graffiti)*

'Why does a woman work ten years to change a man's habit and then complain that he's not the man she married?' *(Barbara Streisand)*

One absent minded vicar forgot the exchange of rings and continued through to the end. When they reached the vestry to sign the registers the worried bride brought it to the vicar's attention. The vicar, who may have been forgetful but was always quick thinking, glossed over the embarrassing hitch by saying: 'Ah yes, of course. This is such a very personal part of the service that I think it is rather nice for us to do this privately together now before we actually sign the registers. Has the best man got the rings ready?'

'Marry her! Impossible! You mean a part of her; he could not marry her all himself. There is enough of her to furnish wives for a whole parish. You might people a colony with her; or give an assembly with her; or perhaps take your morning's walk round her, always provided there were frequent resting-places, and you were in good health.' *(Sydney Smith)*

Once in Cornwall a vicar was officiating at a country village wedding where two farmers were marrying two sisters. It was only when they got to the vestry and had signed the registers that they discovered there had been an awful mix-up and the two farmers were now legally married to the wrong sisters. The vicar, who had never heard of anything like this happening before, got into quite a flap and told them he would have to consult with the registrar to find out what the exact legal procedure would be to rectify the mistake. He told them that on no account should they go home and sleep with the sister they had intended to marry. The two farmers shared a quick exchange and soon settled it between them: "'Tis all right vicar. We don't want no fuss. We'll be sticking to the legal ones now we've got 'em so don't 'e be abothering y'rsen no more!'

Wife: One word out of you and I am going back to my mother.
Husband: Taxi!

A female picked up the phone and heard a repentant voice saying: 'Darling, I'm so sorry. I have been thinking things over and its OK for you to have the Rolls as a little wedding gift – we will move to the South of France and of course you must have your mother to stay with us for as long as you wish. Now will you marry me?'

'Oh darling I certainly will,' came the immediate reply, 'and who is it speaking?'

A vicar who had a reputation for forgetting names and putting in the wrong ones at weddings, devised a formula for avoiding any misunderstandings by announcing at the beginning of the service: 'We are here today to witness the marriage of John and Mary. Be it known unto all present that in the accidental event of any other name being introduced during the course of this service the names John and Mary are always intended . . .'

Q. Did you hear about the dentist who wedded a manicurist?

A. They spent the whole of their marriage fighting tooth and nail!

Steve was an avant-garde painter who married a girl called Helen. After they had been married a few weeks someone asked her how things were going? 'Its wonderful!' she replied. 'Steve paints, I cook; then we try to guess what he has painted and what I have cooked.'

Marriages are made in heaven – but then again so are thunder and lightning

Love is never having to say you're sorry.
Marriage is never having a chance to say anything.

Marriage is a romance in which the hero dies in the first chapter.

The same question posed to three men of God – 'When does life begin?'

The Roman Catholic priest replied: 'At the moment of conception.'

The Anglican clergyman said it was: 'When the child is born.'

As for the Rabbi: 'Ah well,' he said, 'life begins when the children are married, the dog has died and the mortgage has been paid off.'